MW01017352

BEWILDERED RITUALS

BEWILDERED RITUALS

Sandy Shreve

BEWILDERED RITUALS

Published by
Polestar Press Ltd.
P.O. Box 69382, Station K
Vancouver, B.C.
V5K 4W6

Distributed in Canada by
Raincoast Books
112 East Third Avenue
Vancouver, B.C.
V5T 1C8   ·

Published with the assistance of the Canada Council
and the British Columbia Culural Services Branch.

Cover art: *Without Words* by Claire Kujundzic
Cover design by Jim Brennan
Author photo by Bill Twaites
Production by Michelle Benjamin
Printed in Canada

Canadian Cataloguing in Publication Data
Shreve, Sandy
Bewildered rituals
Poems.
ISBN 0-919591-95-7
I. Title
PS8587.H75B49 1992   C811'.54   C92-090558-7
PR9199.3.S47B49 1992 ·

CONTENTS

for Jan O'Brien

"there is no justice we don't make daily"
— Marge Piercy

"what would it mean to stand on the first
page of the end of despair?"
— Adrienne Rich

LEARNING TO READ

for Caitlin Meggs

Words come at us first
as mysterious sounds merged
with the clatter of dishes and flatware
a rustling of leaves or laundry
cupboards and drawers opening, closing...
emerge from a storm of noise
to what a child will hug to her heart
allow to pass her lips
the surprise of one at a time
tentative
then phrases, a sentence
whole paragraphs of expression

The ease of speaking retreats one day
to a mere step toward hieroglyphics
where the a b c's are pronounced
so many different ways
and there is only a map of contradictions
to grasp the magic

Just saying the letters together
never enough to lift familiar sounds
from the page
and a child can get stalled here
anxious for that moment
when books become home
to her eyes, alone

It will not help her to know
we spend our lives
learning to read
Always another new word
interrupts the flow of a good book
the need to read between lines
with no dictionary
for what blank spaces mean

Sometimes the significance
of one cluster of words you might never
see written on paper, anywhere
can haunt a lifetime
elusive as years spent bowing down
to the whip or caress of them
proving them a lie
living up to their truth
or a bit of both, depending

It could be something someone
you love with your life
has said to you
over and over again
thinking it inconsequential
never suspecting
how it's branded to a shape
in your mind, your eye
forever on it, deciphering

WHITER THAN WHITE

this paper is poison
a flat sheet of foolscap
bleached to a concept of cleanliness
fit to kill

its afterbirth bloats rivers and seas
leaches into salmon and seals
turns up in mothers' milk

and milk cartons
made cleaner than clean
the way we're supposed to keep
household ingredients—sheets, shirts,
floors, toilets, tubs
we scrub scrub scrub
flush chemical misconceptions
down the drain

the message assaults our senses:
everything has to be white
including neighbours
colours must sparkle and sheen
like the whiter than whites
compete with pristine northern snow
where an Inuit child suckles dioxins

miles from their origins
in this white-obsessed world
whose palest-skinned race
blanched of pigment
names itself universal
flesh-coloured

where clean is considered
immaculately white
and we finger particles of power
that dissolve to death

DETAIL

Radio interview, March 1988: a Soldier of Fortune *senior editor defends his magazine's policy of encouraging mercenaries to advertise their "skills."*

our cat stares
from the rug on the outside deck
one eye just visible
over the edge of the cedar table
opposite where I sit
a yellow-green glare, wanting in

a hunter, his eyes can be the shade
of sun on those cedar boughs
beyond the porch—a cool colour, even
when leaves are ragged with heat

smoke from my cigarette
twists its way around this room, tension
smooth as purl one knit one purl one
before it dissipates, lost stitches clotted
in the air of my breathing
out of sight

out of mind
as the pesticide-drenched lungs
of whose fingers who picked
the rhubarb and strawberries on the counter
piled high now for preserving, red
bubbling red mass of aromas
sweet smell of condiments, jam
not blood

stains on the editor's hands
he'd calmly call ink
his voice parading the right to kill
into my kitchen, as if it's as ordinary
as breathing or eating
or as the movement I make
to slide open the door for our cat

the announcer paces his program
with a filler: at sunset one evening
a man stuck   *chuckle chuckle*
a picture of his penis on the windshield
of some woman's car

OBJECT LESSON

In Canada one woman is raped every 17 minutes
                —Canadian Association of Sexual Assault Centres, 1981

I sit here wounded from yet another someone's
sense of humour, some cartoonist's idea
of a joke, the cutting edge of hatred
held at my throat
a fist in my eyes as I scanned the calendar stand
for a gift, when the one called "PMS Attack"
jolted my vision to a halt
picture after picture
frame after frame
my womanhood assaulted
again again again

reverberations of women
beaten and raped and murdered
and even as so many women and men mourn
one man can stand up in Senate
cut a swath through debates
with offensive jokes he calls comic relief
in the same breath as he laments
how sometimes it's hard for him
to know what's sexist and what isn't

This kind of hurt burrows deep
gnaws itself into the soul
is a pain that, it seems, must be felt
to be explained

Perhaps men like him would understand
with a bit of visualization
Try reversing the roles
Think for instance of a calendar
"Testosterone Attack" we'll call it
Draw a man in your mind
a stereotype along the lines
of "the dumb hunk" will do
Put him in an elevator
Sketch his testicles like inflated balloons
pinning strangers against the opposite wall
Write the cutline
"I hope no-one notices that my balls are bloated"
and if that makes them laugh
perhaps they need to give it a context
Imagine how this statistic might feel
"in Canada one man is castrated
every 17 minutes"

◊

I return to this poem again and again
searching for an aperture
to release my anger and pain
but the lines close in around my hurt
curled now, like my words
into a fist too close to vengeance
reducing me
to inflicting the same type of wounds
that I want soothed and ended

LOW LEVEL

Imagine a few thousand of these shocks
a season
Out of nowhere
familiar sounds of the day or night
overflown
low
loud

like the shattering boom
he treated us to last spring—
that airforce flyer denounced
'hot dogger'—plane-crazed kid
buzz-bombing the North Shore
caught, of course, in the act
that snatched a lot of hearts
close to attacks
Probably got grounded years
for the show-off stage

He could have gone to Nitassinan
and done it with impunity
No city school-kids, hospital patients,
office executives there to scare—
only Innu and animals

But he didn't—took his toy jet
fighter to what we consider
a populated place
I like to think
maybe he wasn't a hot dog after all
but a rebel: took up his plane
like a pen, brought the impact down
on our heads
so we couldn't ignore it, so when
we read the papers' slight stories
on the Innu protests

we might begin to hear

CHICKEN WINGS

*A found poem, extracted from a CBC "As It Happens" interview with a
U.S. colonel somewhere in eastern Saudi Arabia, Feb. 6, 1991.*

Operation Wing
is an organic chemical detector program
where Buford, the command chicken
is earning his wings
as an all-clear device

Buford and his eleven troopers
don't have to do much—
cluck around camp
gobble handouts
stay in sight of their keepers
so if the birds don't fall down
after scud raids
air quality can be presumed safe
and the soldiers can unmask

The colonel says they chose chickens
over canaries or mice
because they just happened to be handy
He admits they've become camp pets
one of the men has even made
a gas mask for his favourite

this, however, is not considered
a serious threat to the program

RITUALS OF WAR

far from the fighting
we are tangled
in the language of propaganda

transparent turns of phrase
twisted like cats' cradles
for us to inspect and straighten

up against a simplistic truism
that truth
is the first casualty of war

or do people actually nod
as if there is wisdom in this
permission

as though nothing in us dies
each time we reassure our children
over maps and globes

we are safe: here, riddled
with off-beat stories of war
there: that's where weapons shred lives

for whose comic relief do we
wonder at gas masks for poultry
condoms to protect gun barrels from sand

this verbal memorabilia of the absurd
is devastation's thin disguise
yet it feels like there is no end

to the appalling applause for bombs
as the curtains are drawn once more
on what we really know of war

DANCE

this is how the body can move
with grace and fortitude
remember them, two men
to the beat of one drum
their gymnastic limbs swinging
over and under, around
in the soft night air of a park
karate kicks just this far from skin
never come to blows
hands open into air
slow motion, a precision pose
anger transformed to the beautiful
in a dance

in a dance
anger transformed to the beautiful
slow motion, a precision pose
hands open into air
never come to blows
karate kicks just this far from skin
in the soft night air of a park
over and under, around
their gymnastic limbs swinging
to the beat of one drum
remember them, two men
with grace and fortitude
this is how the body can move

SUNSET

one starling chuckles the sun
to crimson down
scavenger of laughter

ACROSS THE ROOM

for Bill Twaites

I watch your fingers
press around a pen
cruise words across the page

a gentle pulse of muscle
ripples your skin smooth, its silk
in lamplight glimmers

Suddenly, just this
is sensuous

each freckle on your forearm
must be kissed

and I
send breathless caresses

MAKING LOVE

making love with you I feel
my body wrap around the earth
a warm cocoon, content long after
making love with you. I feel
at home with everyone all day
cannot imagine indifference after
making love. With you, I feel
my body wrap around the earth

FLIGHT OF THE HERON

out of the still mountains, so close
in this quiet I could touch them

she comes in gentle flight
blue-grey against a pale dawn

the wave of her wings a slow motion
slides past my window

one glance, and she's gone

unfolding a memory of grace
before the city wakens

SURFACES

The hollow scrape of blades
moves skaters through crisp air
this cold, a particular winter
of toques and scarves and gloves
as superfluous as buttons
Jackets flap in the wind
of our movements

So many trajectories
a community singing on ice
the lake almost large enough, people make space
pucks and sticks
pause for these wobbly legs to pass
and no one points to laugh
The only borders here
are where lifeguards hack at the ice
check for thickness and rope off
spots too thin for safety

We slide or glide or stumble
away from treacherous areas
into indiscriminate welcomes
to all who venture onto the lake
this surface beneath our feet
the only skin of concern

In the centre of a city
echoes of unhurried sound
take me back to the Tantramar
redwings in the rushes
their harmonica call a microcosm
of what I miss

What is it about place that seeps
into your soul
mindless of miles, however far you move—
plays out the string and holds you
tempts a false nostalgia
I catch myself believing
this momentary release from rancour
holds the possibility of a city
reclining into country life, as if back home
there was never anything like a frozen pond
abandoned to power, boys
claiming ownership of the top, slap shots
tripping girls' attempts at circles...

At some point every conversation
comments on the relief
of outdoor skating: no one dictating
now to the right, the left,
backward only, just couples,
muzak piping out the pace

Our music is disparate voices
mingled with the language of blackbirds
ducks and crows, our patterns as random
and predictable as their flight ·
Wings slant and turn snug in the sky
feet sculpt curves and crossroads into ice

Such a freeze is rare here—the need
to get to the middle, irresistible
just to see what it's like to look
at the path from the lake for a change

searching for perspective, almost everyone
explores the iced-in cattails and reeds
where the heron hunts when it's water
where we turn from relics of summer
locked in the frozen surface:
styrofoam, cellophane, plastic trash,
lost tennis balls and toys

we look without seeing
how fragile our smiles
when it's youths who feel free
to nod to the aged
whites to the black or the brown
then skate or stroll away
from subtle assumptions behind
who welcomes who

we sing in the same
clutches and gaggles as ever
leaving implications, like litter
for someone else to face

SOLITUDE

smooth flat stones
kisses skim across water
scatter patterns

A PAIR OF WHITE DUCKS

A noose of opaque plastic
Two birds, one trapped in hours
of panic. Feathered waves

Someone's hand tossed that collar
into calm water, cracked
open the can and raised it
to a peaceful evening

a small act
in the scheme of things

like children playing by the lake
daring the speed of their hands
against sprigs of parched grass
lit with matches

it's the flame that gets away
ignites a whole field
It could have been anyone's
and you're indignant
when blamed

just as it isn't you
who's polluted this lagoon
where fishers toss their lines
for trout, imagine
edible fish.

Casting, incessant
as the hoarse mourning
of a lone white duck

SAMHAIN

This night of costumed noise
children masquerade as villains
grinning, more GI Joes than ghosts
this year hold open sacks of hope
we fill up
with UNICEF cents and candy

A bewildered ritual
this 20th-century feast
of the dead
the whistle and blast of firecrackers
enough to chase ancestral spirits
hungry, to their graves

Yet something of the Celts' intent persists
in the last miniature witch
who ascends my steps
with the pride of a priestess

As she passes
the flame inside my pumpkin flickers
an enigmatic wink

TRADITION

*"Crimes ignored sink into the soil like PCBs
and enter the bones of children."*
—Marge Piercy

*"What are trees and gardens to you
When you always speak to the jasmin
With a scythe"*
—Ahmad Shamlou

Dry lightning on a quiet night
scratches the sky with the shapes
of our imagination
Wild abstract designs
and split-second pictures
of skeleton trees
closer to Hallowe'en
than Christmas
when those who can afford to
costume evergreens

Tree farms supply traditionalists
who cannot yet imagine
decorating plastic
and I, among them, arrange exotic
replicas of birds of paradise
to crown the top

Outside my winter window
juncos come with sparrows
forage about the fir and cedar boughs
and sing, free range

an exotic concept for fowl
farmed for our feasting
caged and kept on chemical feed
for rapid growth and slaughter
like cultivated Christmas trees
Both inside my home, permeate
the air I breathe with festive scents
of sap and slowly roasting poultry

BC Means Better Chicken
but the happy poster-hen
will not ride on the transport truck
stacked with her bedraggled cousins

and we will not discuss this
over turkey dinner, next to an evergreen
raised on pesticides toxic to songbirds
that some of us admire and others study
with exacto blades and glue
obsessed with sex and length

Long after dinner
children will curl their fingers
around wishbones
dried for dreams

SEED

the small seed in my hand
paper packages
strewn across the patio like split pods
instructions lost to my careless tearing
irrelevant anyway, it's spring
and I plant in small boxes of soil
composted with hope

these containers will sit
inside a glass house, once again
sprout vegetables and flowers
I'll harvest from my garden
when they've grown

a simple thing, this sowing of a seed
and difficult to think of it as privilege

ODE TO MY TULIP BED

All winter, the bulbous underground
of my garden
plots its pleasure
a clitoral conference of lust
for delight
This sisterhood of passion
has plans for the androgynous sun
a spring display the golden orb
will not resist—
several days of foreplay
warming the slow opening
of bud into succulent love
that will cup and caress
each delicious ray
in velvet ecstasies

Blind voyeurs, we visit
the tulip bed in bloom
admire texture and hue
subtle scent and poise
until we see the five-petalled
scarlet-streaked yellow
has tossed back head and limbs
a full-length stretch
of laughter
exposing everything
down to her deepest delicacy

Enchanted, yet
we name her sensuous power
with the synonyms of our inhibitions
shameless, wanton thing
we say
and wistful, pluck her from
the amorous touch of her lover

place her in a vase
to water our desires

SPRING CLEANING

weeding the files I pretend
the cabinet into a plot of land
as if through this thinning
it will blossom
and everyone who walks in
will admire my new bouquet
lean into each drawer
and breathe deeply the scent
of sorted papers, no longer
ragged edges crammed in every
which way and poised to slash
at skin in vengeance
but petal soft and quivering
to the gentle nudge
of noses seeking fragrance
instead of sneezing dust
now billowing up as I shred
pile after pile of paper
bound for some recycling bin
and bound to come back to me
again in more superfluous copies
to be stuffed and wedged and jammed
into the spaces I've created
for flowers

DUST

returns to touch the surfaces of things
A soft pollen of memory gathers, grey
as dusk, grafts us with its skin of sleep
embracing days with dreams

A soft pollen of memory gathers grey
invisible as ghosts who wander here
embracing days with dreams
particles collect to sheathe my lives

invisible, as ghosts who wander here
layer keepsakes with the stealth of time
Particles collect to sheathe my lives
until my hand picks up the cloth to dust

Layer keepsakes with the stealth of time
a thin shadow before my eyes
until my hand picks up the cloth to dust
around the room I waltz and gently touch

a thin shadow before my eyes
the ceramic ballerina's pose takes hold
around the room, I waltz and gently touch
the friend, who leaving, left for me a dance

the ceramic ballerina's pose   takes hold
as dusk grafts us with its skin of sleep
The friend, who leaving, left for me a dance
returns to touch the surfaces of things

for Kath Beasley

NEIGHBOURS

We discover each other slowly, through
summer afternoons renovating our houses
hear histories between hammer strokes
whose place used to be whose
the school behind the transit line
once a dairy farm
our urban lots the hayfield
until it burned

Newcomers and oldtimers are introduced
grow comfortable with people
who never would have cared to meet
if they hadn't chanced on the same block

We say the same
about most relatives, co-workers
If not for blood or job ties
we'd have nothing in common
let the comment pass as if it's a given
as if proof exists in how easily we lose touch
when we move on
though they change us forever
and we them

A citied-in street slows
the hurry-home from errands
with the syrup of blackberry scent and sweet peas
urging us back toward something
of the country town
a craving for everyone to know everyone
what we've been up to

Fences eventually become supports to lean words on
porches a reason to pause
as we become neighbours for a season
stitching together the remnants of a village
before winter sets in

EYE CONTACT

Days repeat themselves in a grey
weight of clouds, pressed against
her shoulders like a drenched coat
On this street, she reflects
an absence of trees—seems only
a remote flower, a petal
sealed within a bud that spring
keeps missing

I've been striding past her
every day now, for weeks
Each time, my body taut
as thread about to break
as if it will
if I look straight at her
smile and nod when she holds
out her hand for a quarter

I pass into the store
pretend I do not hear
her winced plea
knowing I'll save the change
for her anyway—will come out
head clamped to avoid her glance
drop the silver where I expect
her palm to be

But yesterday, she'd
curled her fingers to her coat
against the cold, and the sound
of money tickling concrete
broke my practiced trance

for an instant, our eyes met awkwardly
Then mine sidled away like thieves
as her gaze spilled to the pavement
to capture metal seeds

FRENZY

for Kate Braid

what happened to our landscapes of desire
our lives like ECGs gone haywire
pen-points zigzag lines way off the page

nothing like our beautiful designs
tasks pop up like weeds that choke
haphazard gardens

untended, we are paper-bound
inside these concrete offices
the line becomes a wire inside a wall

speeds through city streets, our voices
rise along the miles of deadlines, we are
endangered species of ourselves

each call a cry for help transformed
to yet more worthy projects
to complete

where does it end the day insane
extends to sleepless nights
like spinning cartwheels in our minds

people to see
places to go
things to do

list starboard to port with this old joke
like drunkards, our hands grab flowers
as we pass convenience stores

outdoor scents forgotten on our desks
our bleeding fingers greet the next appointment
who notices we chose bouquets of roses

GREEN TEA

I'm told cancer
is being eaten alive
from the inside

when it starts in on the lungs
it feels like a pack
of rats clawing around
gnawing on each sac
sucking up your breath
between incessant bites

Warnings like these
are attempts by friends
to cajole me into quitting smoking

but such campaigns
are as useless
as those caveats I never notice
printed on every pack of cigarettes

They offer nothing so concrete
as the latest possibility
that pots and pots of green tea
will keep me cancer free:
so I sip on this, enjoying
almost every inhalation
of tar and nicotine

CAMEO

From the perspective of this necklace dangling
my jaw must seem like the underside of bellows
Speechless at my throat, she sees

perpetual motion   Streams of air inhaled
exhale incessant sound, depriving her of quiet
From the perspective of this necklace dangling

all is lost to cursory words   Strings of verbs and nouns
spin from my lips, attach to other mouths that
speechless at my throat, she sees

pump phrases into paragraphs, flap
evidence flaccid as ceilings of skin
From the perspective of this necklace dangling

fatigued by my voice, this is no choice performance
She would like to interrupt these wagging chins, but
speechless at my throat, she sees

polemics weave air thick, ossifying language
with thoughtless repetition   She wishes we could listen
from the perspective of this necklace, dangling
speechless at my throat   She sees

WRITER'S BLOCK

for Helen Potrebenko

◊ DETAIL

drape imagination
with the thickness of a rug
inspiration hibernates
inside a frenzy of tasks taken on
shuts creativity up in a closet
heavy with awkward cloth

when I finally sit down
to gather my thoughts
they've gone off on their own
little jaunt
prance around the room
like dust bunnies
dodging the broom

◊ SELF-CENSORSHIP

A woman is blustering her way
into another poem   My opposite
she is wizened, slightly slouched
and enters with all the energy
her anger can muster

brandishing her truth
up and down the aisles of my lines
she topples ideas
with her scythe

until the page is one flattened swath
and she stomps off, leaving me
with the stumps of her interruptions

◊ I, EDITOR

whittle away at verses
chop whole chunks of phrases
chip at words
brush the shavings
off the page

~

whittle
chip at verses
phrases, words

~

whittle words

~

~

◊ EXCUSE

poetry
is a
straight
jacket

I need
a new
form
prose
maybe
but
some
thing
with
more
elbow
room

◊ PRODUCTION LINES

They don't mean to, but prolific writers make me want to
make up a discipline schedule so I can crank out enough
poems to qualify as a *real* writer and when it doesn't work no
matter how much work I do all I get is cranky

Someone once said the best way to deal with writer's block is
to write around it, so I try, circling words as if to round
them up like cattle and fit them into a pen. I do this well.
The problem is getting them out again

Helen tells me there's no such thing as writer's block, and
means it, tells me she just wrote a poem about its absence,
while I'm here writing on and on about what it's like, this
being all I have available when I can't write anything else.
Which might be what she means, that writer's block is
nothing other than having nothing to say, forging ahead just
for the sake of saying something, more is better they say:
praise be, productivity

LONG DISTANCE

they talk long distance   often
chortle whole conversations
house to house giggles
must run in the family, sometimes
all we do is laugh

imagine the telephone lines
bulging through city streets
through trees, belly laughter
bursting back and forth
birds perched on howls of hilarity
bowled over

the instant flight of the vowels
of sound, technological transit
taken for granted as I tap
electronic messages across the country
expect answers

amber flashes on a screen
words threaded through miles
with the unbelievable agility
of hands in a distant land
a woman winds microscopic wires
precisely into pinholes
fingertips meticulous as eyes
strained through a tunnel of lenses

her product the heart of my
hard drive, drives her like a slave
while my fingers pound down
on letters—make invisible waves
the gestures of trans
actions, beyond

belief, the fun I have with this
machine, sometimes it makes my office
like a toybox and I'm the kid
with all the blocks, building
what I want, supposing
I'm in control until it bleeps
resistance

an error message, as if from the woman
working under impositions of silence
on a foreign assembly line
a woman I have never seen
hooks into the long distance feeling
with a programmed distortion
of her scream

TELEPHONE OPERATOR

for Barb Rugo

After a few months
the fluorescent glare
fits her with glasses
she'd never needed
before this job

And she begins to see
her supervisors
as grade school
teachers
from whom permission
for basic functions
must be begged

Even at home
in sleep
when her bladder
shakes her shoulder
from dreams
she wakes to her hand
waving anxiously
in the air

COMPANION

This machine is advertised
as a companion: personal
computer
or perhaps I misunderstand
and the innuendo implies
status

Neither interpretation is real
It takes up space in my office
but it is in fact, mere
mechanical apparatus
a replacement part in the false
hierarchy of jobs

an absence
of someone else's hands
sharing the full range of work
side-by-side with mine

SEX APPEAL

They advertise FDS
for vaginal cleanliness
Certs will certainly ensure
halitosis turning pure
Clairol puts the hair in place
beautifies a homely face
flabby bums are guaranteed
held snug, rotund, in Levi jeans

With passion pounding at my gut
a glut, I gulp the ads—my mind
enshrines a ready-mix of jingles
Singles out a products-plan
with which I'll surely catch a man!

But nightly how I do despair
aware that should he share my bed
instead of facing "femme fatale"
the flawed and awful me he'll see

"DID YOU COME?"

"Don't worry about it if you didn't come," he said, "most women don't their first time." "Oh...okay," she said, thinking "whew, gee he's so understanding, so sweet," just milliseconds after her first response whispered through her mind, "wow, you mean there's *more*, this wasn't *it*, I can't wait, let's do it again and see!" but being no expert on sex, having just lost her virginity, she listened to his elaboration, "y'know, some women never have orgasm and you might be one of these," and it never occurred to her to tell him *she* thought she'd had one because what did she know about these things, and besides he'd fallen asleep. "Did you come?" the next man in her life asked, the first one having left for another virgin to confuse, "oh, yes," she said, "it was wonderful," though she didn't but he seemed convinced so her body was probably just wrong again. "You're the tallest woman I've ever made love to," the next one declared, "did you come?" "No," she said, now thoroughly uncertain as to how men thought she should display this event, "oh, I was sure you did," he said, dejected. "Did you come?" she asked the new man, before he could ask her first

CYCLE

For now, the sun has crashed
the gates of last night's rain
We are the lovers of dawn
thrive on early rising to emerge
from drowsy houses—leave the sleepers
to their dreams, we spin
through morning mist and willow green
and I, for one, haunt this park
with longing

This small hour a fantasy
to follow my breath, wherever
peddle my desires to herons in the trees
Widgeons grazing in the grass
take flight at each arrival
whistle from the sun-striped lake
until we pass

We, who come to sip of peace, unwitting
cause the birds' routine
of fearful feeding
But I'll think no more of contradictions
fling my mind to flight with sea gulls
gather canvasses of clouds
Off-key as the crows, I compose
symphonies of freedom

even as I leave
duty driven to my day
the ghost of myself remains
there, just past that clump of reeds
bursting with the crescendo
of redwings

WALKING BACK TO SACKVILLE

Picnics at Fort Beauséjour
conjured nightmares
ransacked casemates
bayonets at my back
everyone running through
narrow corridors
crumbling walls
cannons
the incessant pound
of my heart
powdered air
the dry scream
in my throat

until there is only me
stumbling across the marsh
desperate to catch up to the sound
of my voice

◊

Along an abandoned track
weeds flourish, tar-scented ties
fumble with footsteps
until I slow my pace
to centimeters less than
anxiety

to get there   Miles ahead
there is a museum
I can never find in daylight
The rail line somehow reaches
out of the marsh to a crossroad

and the old stone building looms
grey and ornate
inviting me in just
before closing

I race from floor to floor
seeing nothing

Walking back to Sackville
a companion I meet on the tracks
explains
in a language foreign only
to me

◊

On the high marsh steel girders
rise, scaffolding the chamomile air
a rust-red invasion
of the land that inhabits me
bulges tumours
beside concrete clover-leaves

I want nothing to do with this
my heart constricts
breathheld
I wake

years in the city
later, this
is the dream that taunts

◊

Fighting my way back

I am a blister in the wind
abandoned on a grassy rampart
steep above the highway

an ending
in the middle of the marsh

DULSE

tastes just this side of bitter
paper thin and purple, I savour
its salt-air flavour
much to my husband's disgust
how can you eat that stuff!
my fishy kisses
greeted with suspicion
so I exile myself
to the opposite side of the room
defiantly feast
on an insignificant cultural gap
vast as a continent
between us

OUT OF SEASON

Beneath a street lamp, the soft chaos
of snowflakes falling, as they nudge themselves
between gusts of air like a picture
of someone breathing

then driven straight against their inclination
into angled arrows, they are weapons
of a wind that comes up out of nowhere
as if to ridicule
the stubborn faith of people here
in out-of-season rain gear

I cannot adapt myself
to umbrellas in the snow
a hopeless coastal habit of denial
or is it resistance to lingering winter
and in my condescension of mere difference
have I missed their February sense of it

that tomorrow will bring rain poking holes
in the feeble snow, for crocuses

SNOW SESTINA

for Maggie Benston

The mountain doffs its cap of cloud
to the dazzling art of snow
and standing here with all this in my eyes
I breathe in several degrees below
zero, up to my knees in powder
a breeze caressing my face

I cannot begin to fill my eyes
with the clarity of winter air   Here below
the sudden frescoes of snow
miles distant, I feel face to face
with those sweeping strokes of powder
paintings, fallen from a cloud

This morning sounds like powder
floating in the air   Just below
the stillness of a willow cloaked in snow
I bend to form an angel out of cloud
that's landed here to cool my face
and tantalize my eyes

It sparkles crystalline, this eau de snow
melting on my mitten, scents my face
the one perfume I'll wear, a dab of cloud
here, on my forehead, neck and just below
each ear, each touch as soft as powder
puffs, swift as the blink of eyes

The beauty of geometry in snow
is like a poem and the grin on your face
when I said I loved the math in words—cloud
covered thoughts unveiled like equations, eyes
opened to shifting solutions, below
above and around each phrase, whimsical as powder

in a wind, images and ideas to create, then face
and balance as best I can—the way snow
can be both flurry and blizzard, powder
and firm, a pleasure to the eyes
and agony for skin, glowering in a pewter cloud
while lighting up night on the ground below

The mountains flaunt white powder, while below
city dwellers' eyes are on the sky, dread any cloud
that delivers more snow than we know how to face

MORE CLOUD AND SHOWERS

for Meredith Kimball

"...the place we end up in
goes deeper than choice, if we're lucky."
—Bronwen Wallace

Just when I think I've had
all the rain I can take
the concept of drought
a sodden longing, reluctant
I tread toward aqueous origins
slosh along sidewalks
water on the mind, the sound
of it gushes down drainpipes
a constant thought
waterlogged, I have forgotten
the taste of thirst
mere rumour

it seems impossible to imagine
people who draw calm
and comfort from this climate
they are the incomprehensible other
secretly lifting their faces
in quiet places, in praise
of drizzle and deluge

for the rest of us
rain is another word for bleak
we can only distinguish
one shade of grey sky
lush rainforest greens
invisible to our eyes
flowers droop with the weight
of wet

everything we do
defined by daily forecasts
for more cloud and showers
rotting the tentative seams
of our lives
jobs dissolve
lovers touch and draw tears
we are so bloated
with this weather
we are ready to accept death
by drowning
or move

Just when we think we've had
more than enough
a wind comes up
erases the shroud
mountains emerge like a hug
flowers admit to petals
strut their stuff for the sun

and we bask in it
dry at last
every tear appears mended
with the invisible stitching
of Sulis
we are transformed
to a magic patchwork of glee
lotus land lovers again
incapable of leaving

which is why anyone stays
anywhere, really
if they have the fortune
of choice:
for their own moments
of glorious hope

FOG HORN

for my sisters, Janet and Carolyn

Hidden in sunshine rushes
a heron's fog horn warning
pulls me back to a St. Croix cottage
summers spent priming the pump
of solitude, ice-water swims and rock shore walks
extended family gatherings and verandah chat
galore   When the mist rolled in
on echoes of laughter across the water
all the children clamoured
for a turn at the metal grey funnel
honoured to empty our lungs
for the sake of caution
knowing any boater would welcome
the familiar atonal call

Morning in this park a calm descends
with the warmth   My book says
the heron sounds her alarm
with several hoarse squawks, but just now
the calls are single, almost soft

the way a child tries the fog horn
for the first time, in sunshine

Trout Lake, Vancouver—1990

WHALE WATCHING

for Andrea Lebowitz

All week we search through sightings
of seals and otters
and lost logs in the water
for the orcas

Hoping to see fins in the distance
binoculars raised
we whisk our eyes across wave
after wave, wish away the constant
ferries and outboards
want the channel a calm
invitation for whales

as if our seeing them
would be proof of possibility
that all we have inflicted
on this world
might be reversed
and all the ruin changed
to an unscathed grace

as if the common seal
no longer counts enough for this
approaches going home
with a story of sea gulls
instead of eagles

Do we want the rare, endangered
species to visit us
to bestow some special privilege
like a trust
that tells us we are not
the culprits

I want to believe it's something else
this longing for the exotic
something that transcends
such tired desires

Of course, the time comes
when we give up
accept a pattern of metallic slaps
as one more shipping sound
Engrossed in books we let it pass
until by accident of a glance
we glimpse the last three whales
breaching in the bay just yards away

We gaze, trapped between elation and regret
in that moment luck has granted—
kicking ourselves for what we missed
we still feel honoured by the orcas
who likely neither know nor care
that we are, wistful, there
wishing they'd come back
give us one more chance

in memory of

Maggie Benston

&

Bronwen Wallace

NOTES ON THE TEXT

The opening quotation is by Marge Piercy from her poem "The Ram's Horn Sounding" in Available Light; *the one by Adrienne Rich is from her poem "Dreams Before Waking" in* Your Native Land, Your Life.

p. 22, Dance *is a palindrome, "a word, sentence, or verse which reads the same either backwards or forwards."*

p.25, Making Love *is an unrhymed triolet, "one of the French fixed forms of verse... Containing only two rhymes, the triolet has a total of eight lines: the first two are repeated as the last two; the fourth is the same as the first. The rhyme scheme is thus abaaabab."*

p. 32, Samhain: *"...All Hallows Eve, the original night-time festival...when the 'crack between the worlds' could open up and let the spirits pass through. Therefore the ghosts of dead ancestors could revisit the earth, join their descendants at the feast, and give necromantic interviews and omens...[T]he church...insisted that demons were abroad on Halloween, summoned by witches, which was the usual term for the ancient pagan priestesses whose business it was to communicate with the dead."*
—Barbara G. Walker, The Woman's Dictionary of Symbols & Sacred Objects.

pp. 33-4, Tradition: *The Marge Piercy quote is from her poem "Slides from our recent European trip" in* Available Light; *the Ahmad Shamlou quote is from his poem "The Game Is Over," in* Spirits of the Age *(ed. Mona Adilman).*

Scientists curious about the mating patterns of swallows cut the tails of some males and used the tips to elongate the tails of others only to find that females sought those with the longest tails for sex, whether or not they were already mated.

p. 39, Dust *is an unrhymed pantoum, a "Malayan verse form...[with] an indefinite number of stanzas, each consisting of a quatrain rhyming abab. The second and fourth lines of each stanza become the first and third lines of the next. In the last stanza, the second and fourth lines are the first and third lines of the opening stanza reversed; thus, the poem ends with the same line with which it began."*

p. 44, Cameo *is an unrhymed villanelle, a French fixed form with "five tercets followed by a quatrain, all on two rhymes. The opening line is repeated at the ends of tercets two and four; the final line of the first tercet concludes the third and fifth. The two refrain lines are repeated at the end of the quatrain."*

pp. 63-4, Snow Sestina: *"...the sestina originated in medieval Provence. It has six unrhymed stanzas, in which the terminal words of each line are repeated in varying orders, followed by a tercet (a unit of three lines) which may include three of the terminal words or all six, used two to a line."*

pp. 65-6, More Cloud and Showers: *The Bronwen Wallace quote is from her poem "Seeing Is Believing" in* The Stubborn Particulars of Grace; *Sulis is the Celtic sun goddess.*

Definitions are from A Reader's Guide to Literary Terms, *Ken Beckson and Arthur Ganz.*

ACKNOWLEDGEMENTS

Some of these poems have appeared or are forthcoming in the following publications:

Alberta Poetry Yearbook
AUCE Provincial News
Books in Canada
Contemporary Verse 2
Canadian Physicians for the Prevention of Nuclear War Quarterly
event
Guardian (HEU)
It Was, It Was Not: Essays & Art on the War Against Iraq (ed. M. Briemberg)
More Than Our Jobs (eds. G. Downie, P. Tranfield)
Paperwork (ed. T. Wayman)
The Pottersfield Portfolio

Some of these poems have been broadcast on CBC's "Art Beat" and on Vancouver Co-operative Radio's "Red Eye" and "Union Made." "Whiter Than White" was published as a broadsheet by the Vancouver Industrial Writers' Union for National Book Week, 1991. "Sex Appeal" was awarded first prize for humour in the 1980 Alberta Poetry Contest.

I am grateful to many friends for their support and encouragement, and in particular to Kate Braid, Susan Eisenberg, Kathy Fretwell, Nick Witheford and Colleen Wood for their thoughtful comments on various stages of the manuscript. Special thanks to Bill Twaites, Star Rosenthal and Michelle Benjamin.

MORE POETRY FROM POLESTAR PRESS

Marie Annharte Baker
BEING ON THE MOON
Winner of the 1990 City of Regina Book Award

Kate Braid
COVERING ROUGH GROUND
Winner of the 1991 Pat Lowther Memorial Award

George Elliott Clarke
WHYLAH FALLS
Winner of the Archibald Lampman Poetry Award

Glen Downie
AN X-RAY OF LONGING

Mona Fertig, editor
LABOUR OF LOVE:
AN ANTHOLOGY OF POETRY ON PREGNANCY AND CHILDBIRTH

Jim Green
NORTH BOOK
*Winner of the Canadian Authors Award and the
Alberta Award for Poetry*

Paulette Jiles
THE JESSE JAMES POEMS

Bill Richardson
QUEEN OF ALL THE DUSTBALLS AND OTHER EPICS
OF EVERYDAY LIFE

Allan Safarik
ON THE WAY TO ETHIOPIA

Allan Safarik, editor
VANCOUVER POETRY

Dale Zieroth
THE WEIGHT OF MY RAGGEDY SKIN